Leo's
Big Bed Adventure:

Learning to Sleep All by Myself!

Written by Geraldine Dayan
Illustrated by Lícia Andrade

With Love and Gratitude

To my two greatest inspirations, my little lights who brighten my days —my beautiful children, Emma Joyce and Abraham Meir. Thank you for teaching me, without words, to be a better person every day and for filling my life with endless joy.

To my dear husband Daniel Geller and loving parents Monica and Alberto Dayan, your unwavering support, wisdom, and encouragement have shaped me in more ways than I can express. Thank you for teaching me the value of kindness, the strength in perseverance, and the courage to chase my dreams.

A special thank you to my wonderful mother-in-law, Janete Geller, for her invaluable help in editing this book and making it even more magical for children.

Above all, I thank G-d for blessing me with the gift of life, family, love, and the ability to bring this story to fruition. May this book bring warmth, joy and lots of laughter to all who read it.

In a cozy little town, there lived a happy family: Mommy, Daddy, and their little boy, Leo.

Every night, Leo would snuggle into his bed with his favorite teddy bear, Berry. Mommy would sing sweet songs, and Leo would fall asleep with a big, happy smile on his face.

But one cold winter night, a chilly breeze woke Leo up. *"Hmm… maybe I'll go cuddle with Mommy and Daddy!"* he thought.

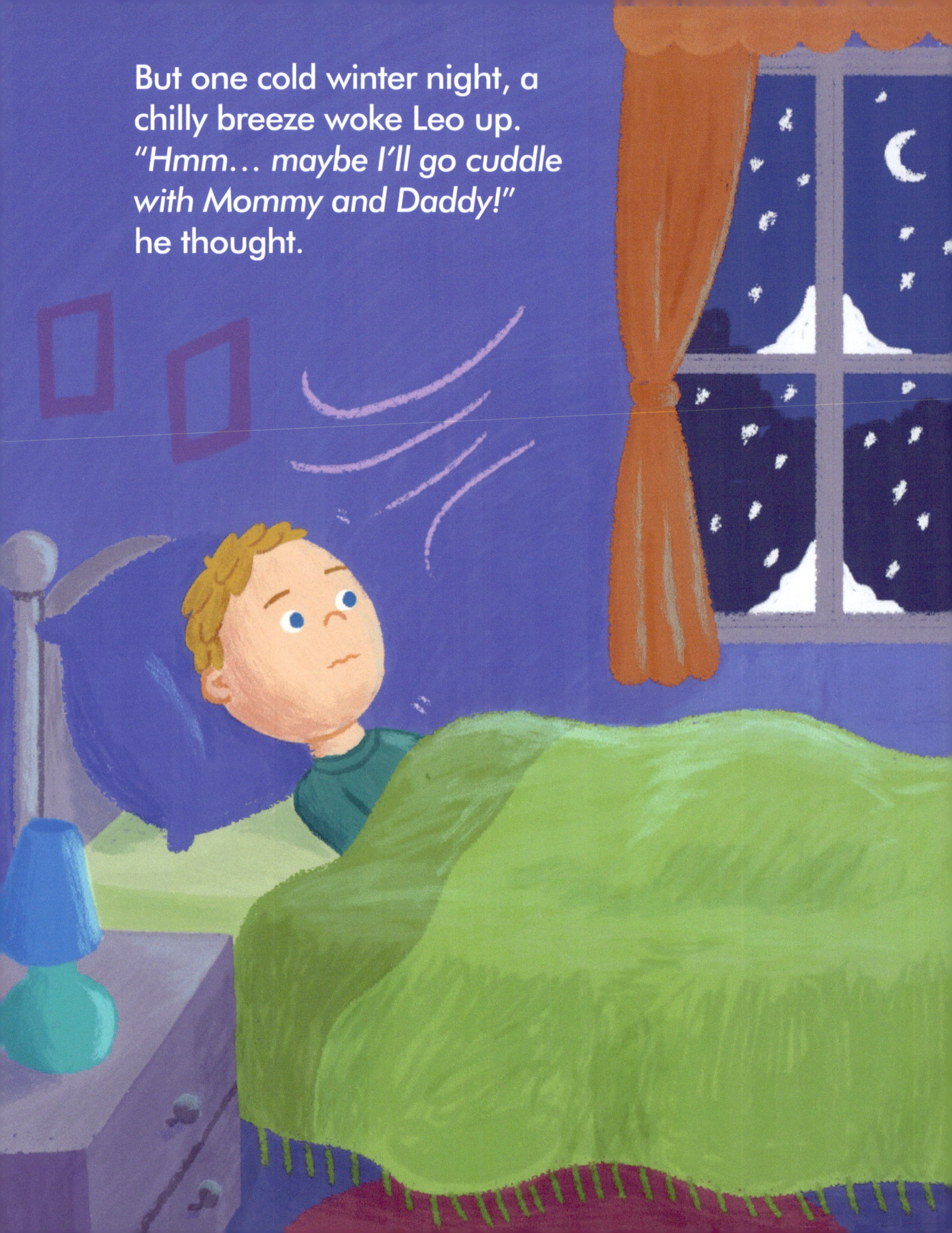

So he tiptoed to their room, climbed into bed between them, and snuggled in.

But suddenly…
Mom started **tossing and turning**!
She squished Leo without even realizing
he was there!

"Mom, Mom!" Leo whispered. "Please don't squish me like a pancake! I'm trying to sleep!"

"Oh, Dear!" said Mama, with a sleepy smile. "Would you like to go back to your own bed? I'm sure no one will squish you like a pancake there!

But Leo loved being in his parents' room, so he simply snuggled in and went back to sleep.

All was calm again, until…
Daddy's BIG BOOOOOMING
snores filled the room!

ZZZZ

"Daddy, could you please try not to snore so loudly? It's hard for me to sleep" Leo asked.

Daddy chuckled. "Oh, buddy, when grown-ups sleep, sometimes they make funny noises - Maybe your cozy little bed is the best place for some nice and quiet sleep".

Leo giggled and lay down again, but before he could fall asleep…

Mommy sneezed a huge sneeze!

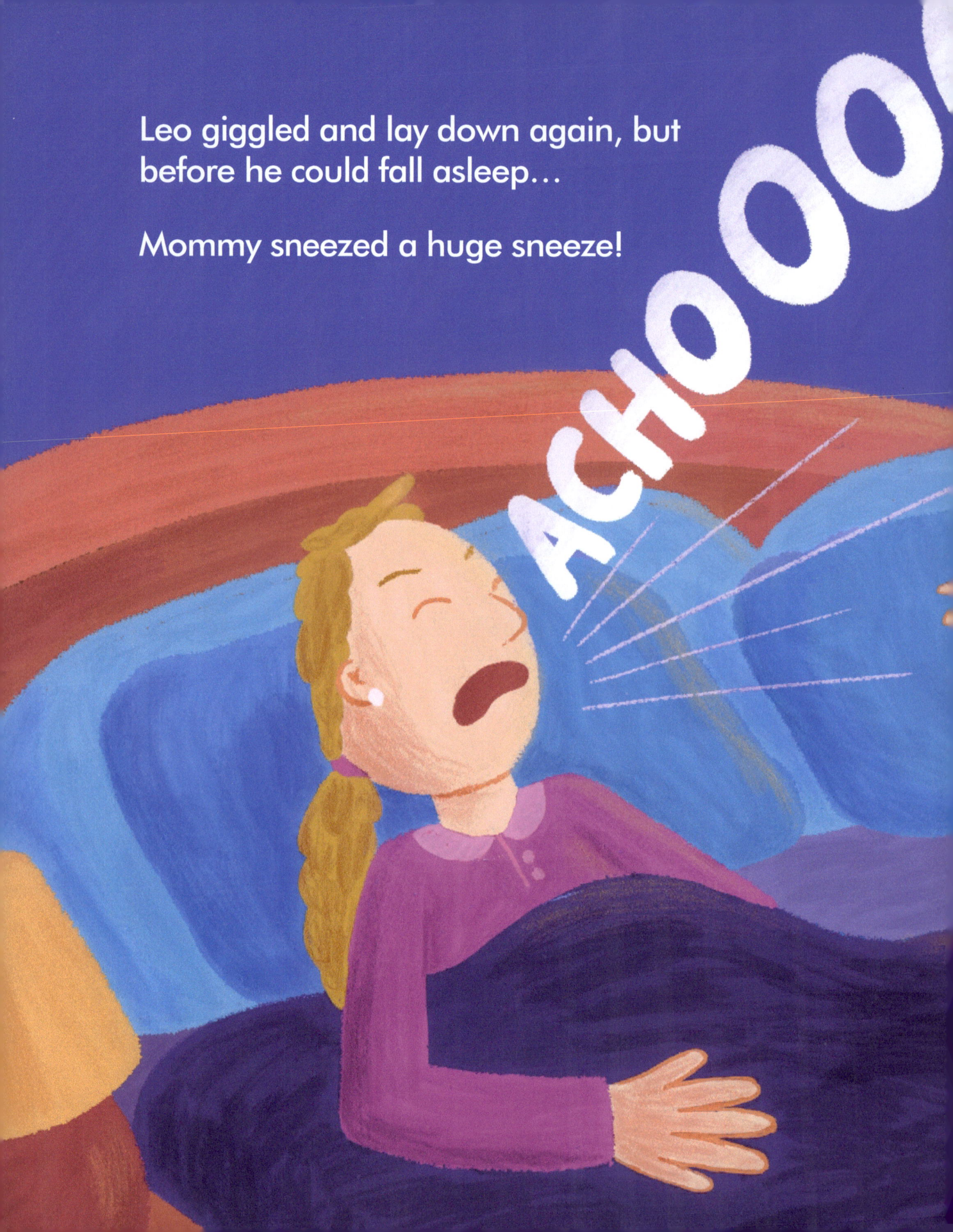

ACHOOOOO!

"Mommy! Your sneeze almost blew me out of bed!" Leo exclaimed.

"Oh, sweetie," Mommy said, "Sneezes happen sometimes! But I promise, if you go back to your bed, there will be no sneezes to blow you away!"

Leo sighed and snuggled back in, hoping
for some sleep at last.
But just as he was falling asleep…

SNIF
SNIF

Sniff, sniff…
A strange smell filled the air.
Leo wrinkled his nose. "Uh-oh…"

Mom and Leo both looked at each other,
gasping and waving their hands.
"Ewwww! What is that smell?"

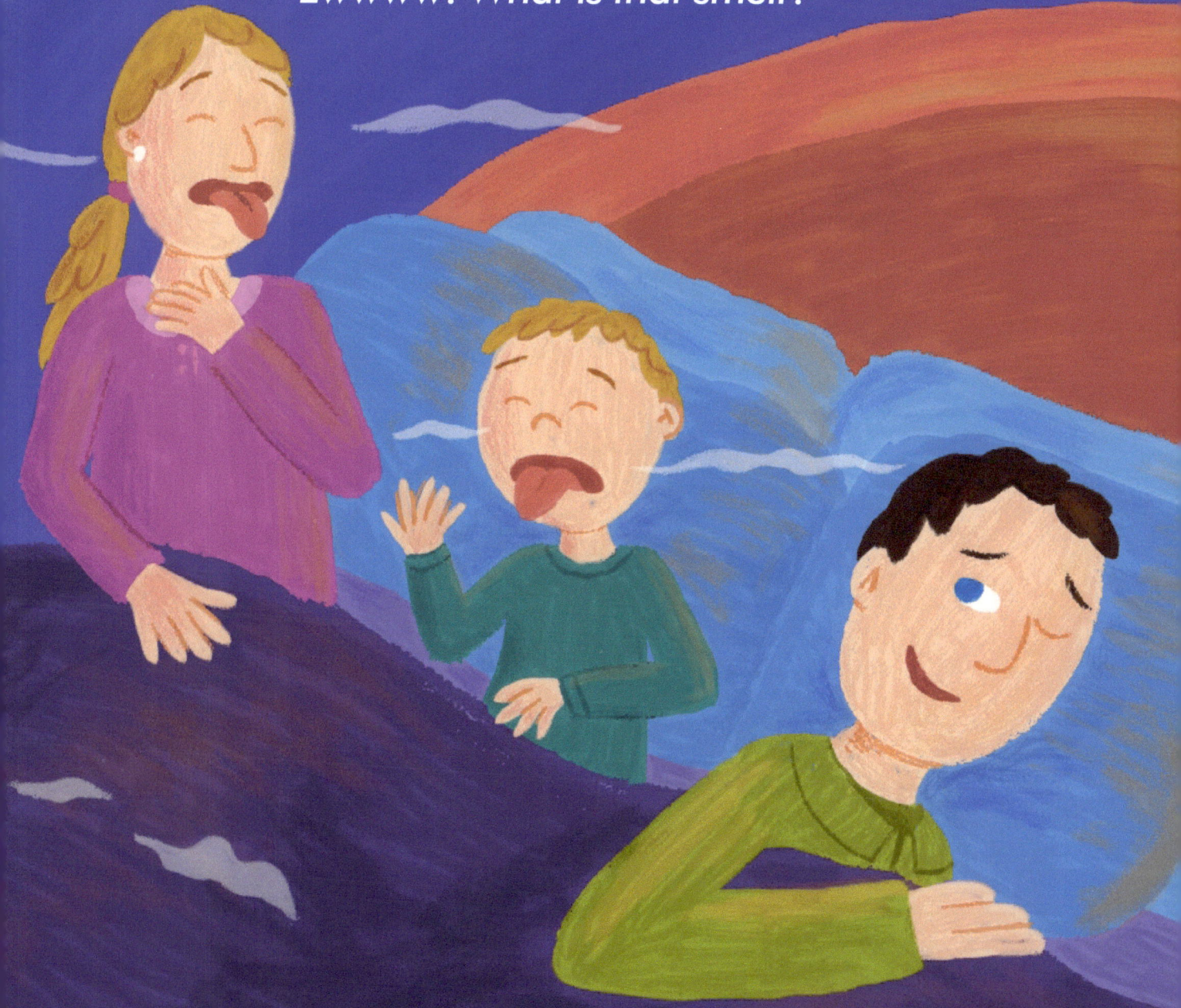

Dad opened one eye, looking a bit sleepy.
"Oops... sorry! That was just a little 'Dad surprise'.

Leo shook his head, giggling but exhausted.

That night, he realized that as much as he loved his parents and loved cuddling with them, **it was time for him to learn how to sleep on his own.**

He tiptoed back to his room
and climbed into his cozy bed
next to his teddy bear Berry.

Leo now understood that his bed was truly the
best place to be. It was warm and comfy - *free
of tossing, snoring, sneezes, and funny smells!*
He felt like a big boy, sleeping alone in his own
bed. Above all, he felt safe, knowing that no
matter where he slept, his parents' love would
always shine on him - like stars glowing softly
through the night.

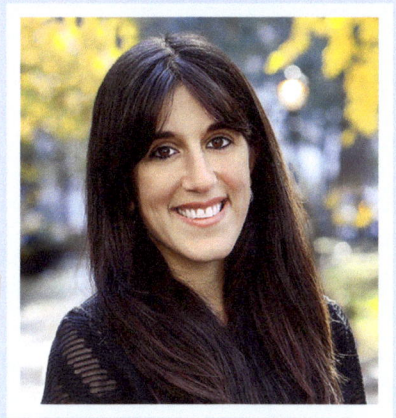

About the Author

Born in Argentina, Geraldine Dayan moved to Florida at the age of 14 and later pursued her studies in New York, graduating magna cum laude with a degree in finance. Though her career led her into the world of business and real estate, her passion for working with children has always been a constant in her life. Throughout her teenage years, she tutored younger kids in mathematics and English and worked in Montessori schools, dedicating years to nurturing young minds and fostering a love of learning.

Her greatest inspiration, however, comes from home - every night, she tells stories to her own children, filling their imaginations with warmth and wonder. It was these treasured bedtime moments that led her to write her first children's book. Geraldine's journey to motherhood was one of strength and perseverance. After experiencing multiple miscarriages, she developed an even deeper empathy for others and a profound appreciation for the magic of childhood. Through her writing, she hopes to bring comfort, joy, laughter, and a sense of security to little readers and their families.

She currently lives in Florida with her husband and children, embracing both the adventure of family life and the joy of storytelling.

Contact: geridayan@gmail.com | Instagram: @geridayan

About the Illustrator

Lícia Andrade is an illustrator from São Paulo, Brazil. She began her professional journey as an architect and urban planner, graduating from Mackenzie Presbyterian University. Throughout her career, she worked primarily in residential projects, interior design, and various renovations - including shops and factories - where she collaborated in the production of technical drawings.

Although passionate about architecture, Lícia eventually chose to shift paths, seeking a more playful and imaginative outlet for her creativity. Drawing had always been a part of her life - from a young age, she loved creating her own stories and characters. This deep-rooted love for artistic expression led her to embrace illustration as her true calling. Lícia has since illustrated children's books published both in Brazil and internationally. Her artistic voice brings warmth and storytelling to every project she touches.

Beyond illustration, one of her favorite pastimes is playing piano. Music inspires her imagination, often sparking new visual ideas. She also enjoys watching films and analyzing the narrative structures, which feed her passion for crafting compelling visual stories.

Contact: licia.andrade.r@gmail.com
Instagram: @liandradeilustra

www.ingramcontent.com/pod-product-compliance
Lightning Source LLC
Chambersburg PA
CBHW040749100426
42735CB00034B/126